GOD AND I:
OUR CONVERSATIONS

GOD AND I:
OUR CONVERSATIONS

NEELAM CHALLONER

WIPF & STOCK · Eugene, Oregon

Wipf and Stock Publishers
199 W 8th Ave, Suite 3
Eugene, OR 97401

God and I
Our Conversations
By Challoner, Neelam
Copyright©2019 Apostolos
ISBN 13: 978-1-5326-8106-6
Publication date 2/2/2019
Previously published by Apostolos, 2019

Unless otherwise stated, all scripture quotations are from the are taken from The One New Man Bible, copyright © 2011 William J. Morford. Used by permission of True Potential Publishing, Inc. Scripture quotations marked "TLV" are taken from the Tree of Life Translation of the Bible, copyright © 2015 by The Messianic Jewish Family Bible Society. Scripture quotations marked "MSG" are taken from The Message, copyright © 1993, 1994, 1995, 1996, 2000, 2001, 2002. Used by permission of NavPress Publishing Group. Scripture quotations marked "ESV" are taken from the ESV Bible (The Holy Bible, English Standard Version®), copyright © 2001 by Crossway, a publishing ministry of Good News Publishers. Used by permission. All rights reserved." Scripture quotations marked "AMP" are taken from The Amplified Bible, copyright © 2015 by The Lockman Foundation, La Habra, CA 90631. All rights reserved. For Permission To Quote information visit http://www.lockman.org/. Scripture quotations marked "NKJV" are taken from the New King James Version®, copyright © 1982 by Thomas Nelson. Used by permission. All rights reserved.

Contents

Acknowledgements 6

Introduction 7

Prologue..9

Encounter with My Creator 13

The Sapphire and the Warrior Part One 21

The Sapphire and the Warrior Part Two 26

Love in the Storm 33

Ectopic Episode 39

Moving My Mountain 45

My Promised Land 51

My Mirror 59

My Prayer 67

A Royal Invitation 73

Epilogue...80

Acknowledgements

I give thanks and glory to God-YHWH, for without my conversations with Him my life would not have been shaped and fashioned. I praise Him for inspiring me to author a book. You are my Light and my Salvation.

To Gary, my love, my husband, my friend, my perfect match, thank you for always supporting me and believing in me. We've been through much and yet there is still more of the glory realm to tap into.

To Gwen for praying for me and calling me with words of encouragement, when I least expected them, but when I needed them most. Thank you to our fellowship and my friends for love and support and to Mathew Bartlett, Chris Hammond and Sue Portman who helped me put this book together, I truly appreciate you.

Thank you to Shaneen Clarke , you connected me to Jesus, He is my best friend, my first Love. And thank you for being bold and yet humble when sharing the gospel of Gods salvation to my father's household.

To my late father, thank you for your vision and affirmation to us children saying "You are the best ". We shall rejoice together in Zion.

To you, the reader, may this book inspire a divine dialogue with the Most High, touch your soul and stir your spirit. May you begin life-changing conversations with God, Who is the Great I AM.

Neelam

Introduction

Why this book?

"What do you want me to do?" This is a question I ask God on a regular basis. It could be prompted by a particular situation or time, or simply a request for guidance. I was working out on my cross trainer one morning, and in my heart I was asking God my Father this question. That was when the inspiration for this book came to me. I felt compelled to share how God has been so important, relevant and evident in my life. I heard an answer – a voice – rise up from within me, "Write and testify what I have done – share this with others." Somehow, I knew, without a shadow of doubt, this was to become *God and I: Our Conversations*.

I knew that this did not come from me, but from the Holy Spirit – and here I am, writing this book under divine inspiration, as a message that God is real, and He talks and walks with those who call upon Him.

The purpose of this book is simply to describe my experience with God and His hand upon my life. To share our intimate moments, our conversations. I am a seeker and the questions in my heart are always answered.

> *One thing have I desired of the LORD, that will I seek after; that I may dwell in the house of the LORD all the days of my life, to behold the beauty of the LORD, and to enquire in his temple. Psalm 27:4 (ONM)*

God has done many things in my life, but I have selected a few key conversations and seasons to share with you.

My prayer is that you will open your heart and mind to the possibility that God exists, that you will also experience Him in a tangible way, and if you haven't already, you'll receive the gift of salvation that comes from Yeshua-Jesus Christ, who said, "I am the Way, the Truth and the Life; no one comes to the Father, except through Me" (John 14:6).

The purpose of sharing my conversations is to help every reader understand that God is a living Being who speaks, listens, answers our call, guides us, instructs us, and that most importantly His plan for us is good, always good, because He is Love.

Religion, I now understand, was not God's plan or idea – religion was man's creation. God's redemptive plan to bring man back to Himself was His intention right from the time when Adam and Eve sinned in the garden of Eden. We were created and designed to worship and be intimate with God, so it's in our natures to know and worship Him. As His creation, God gave us one thing above His angels, and that is free will. We have a choice to follow Him or not.

There are not many ways to God as I previously thought – there cannot be many truths can there? There is only one God. This inconvenient truth led me to "The Way."

Prologue

But we have the same spirit of faith, according to what is written, "I believed, and therefore I spoke." So we also believe, and therefore we also speak ... as we look not at what can be seen but at what cannot be seen. For what can be seen is temporary, but what cannot be seen is eternal. 2 Corinthians 4:13 & 18 (TLV)

We're not keeping this quiet, not on your life. Just like the psalmist who wrote, "I believed it, so I said it," we say what we believe.... There's far more here than meets the eye. The things we see now are here today, gone tomorrow. But the things we can't see now will last forever." 2 Corinthians 4:13 & 18 (MSG)

About 1983, I was around 7 or 8 years old, when late one evening, my Mama-Granny (my father's mum) came to stay the night. Granny sat at the dining room table, leaning against the wall. She had her scarf around her head as she usually wore it. As she and my mum were chatting away in Punjabi, Granny kept looking at me, so I knew that I was the subject of the conversation. I think I was sitting on the carpet, listening carefully, and although I didn't understand everything, I knew the meaning of some of the words.

Later Mum explained what she had said: "One day she's going to be a strong woman of God." I poured over religious Hindu books from a very young age, and my openness to following my Hindu religion was evident – Granny felt my hunger was a sign from God.

Sometime in my teens, my other Nan (mum's mum) said to my mum, "Neelam's got something. Whatever she says it comes true." I am not sure if I was there when she said this as the conversation would have been in Punjabi again. But if I was present, I know how the scenario would have played out. Nan would have sat on the sofa observing me, as she always did on her many visits, quietly watching and contemplating her thoughts and what she was seeing.

Mum told me what she had said many years later and we understood she had meant that I had a gift, a spiritual gift, as described in the Bible – perhaps a prophetic gift.

CHAPTER ONE

Encounter with My Creator

You must regularly ask and it will be given to you, you must continually seek and you will find, you must knock habitually and it will be opened to you. For everyone who asks, takes, and the one who seeks, finds, and it will be opened for the one who knocks. Matthew 7:7-8 (ONM)

My father was one of seven brothers and four sisters, and as a family we were strongly united. My memories of growing up in my grandparents' home and the closeness we shared are precious and vivid to this day.

From June 1992 onwards, we suffered several tragedies. One of my uncles passed away, one of my dad's younger brothers, a young and talented non-conformist, with whom I was close. I recall many animated and passionate conversations with him about life, family and about his dreams and promises. He was in a well-known Bhangra band, playing the Dholki-Indian two-sided drums, so his legacy lives on through music as well as the memories. The loss and grief I felt was great, as it was for the whole family, and especially his wife and three young boys who felt lost and confused, in shock as their world turned upside down in an instant. His eldest son, although in his early teens at the time, once he accepted the loss and came to terms with the situation, felt an overwhelming sense of responsibility towards his family, and I imagine he still does. My uncle's death shook our family to the core, he was so young and so much loved. The funeral was on my eighteenth birthday, but as you can imagine, that year I never celebrated.

Just four weeks later one of my aunts died suddenly, also at a very young age. She was the younger sibling of my aunt who had just been widowed. Her life was just beginning when, unexpectedly, she was gone. I remember admiring her whenever she did her hair and makeup at my grandparents' home. I kept thinking, "one day I can get dressed up like her." She was bold and beautiful and like me, petite. My aunty had given birth to her third child and left behind her new-born and two very young children. As a family, we were still in mourning from my uncle passing away and now with this sudden loss we were in inexpressible pain.

Just a few months later, her husband, another uncle, passed away. Like his brother, he was a talented drummer who often played with bands. I remember him tapping his hand on many different surfaces even the dashboard of his car to any beat or making up his own. He had amazing big curly hair it was like an afro, I think this set him apart from his brothers; well that is what I always thought, and still do. Being so young too, his dreams went with him yet, he left three beautiful children. My widowed aunt immediately took my baby cousin in, and her three boys now had a new baby sister. I guess my aunt now felt a different sense of purpose and responsibility. Although grief-stricken and managing the giant void in her life, I imagine she felt in the baby an echo of her late sister's presence. My younger cousins were at the main family home with two of dad's youngest brothers and my grandmother. It was their home, and stability and a sense of normality was vital at such tender ages.

Soon after, bereft with the grief of losing two sons and a daughter-in-law so suddenly, my grandmother passed away too. I cannot describe what we were going through as a whole family, and to be honest I wouldn't attempt it, each person has their own way of dealing with loss and grief. The pain, even to this day, is deep. The loss bought us closer and has shaped how we are to this day as a family. The memories and legacy of each family member lives on in our hearts.

Early one Saturday morning that year, shortly after my uncle had passed away, there was a knock at the door. We had attended a family event the night before, so the whole household, my parents, my younger sisters and I, were asleep. I heard my dad get up and go to the window, then urge my mum, "Get up and answer the door." He said to her that he had seen the visitors before in a dream. Mum opened the door and invited the couple in. They were an Asian Christian couple who came to offer their condolences and share the gospel of Jesus.

By the time I was fully awake and went downstairs a couple of hours later, my parents were still talking with our visitors over tea and biscuits. I didn't really get involved with their conversation but I didn't mind that they were there. The wife, whose name I learned was Shaneen, was really friendly and seemed to connect with me. After that day, my mum and my sisters began going to church, which, again, I didn't mind, but Christianity was not for me. Several months went by with Mum attending church regularly and Dad joining her as and when he could. I couldn't deny the change in both my mum and dad and to the atmosphere in our home. While it caught my attention, I still resisted. My resistance to Jesus and the Bible caused strife in the home, and led me to rebel against my parents.

I recall arguments where I would say to them, "Don't Bible-bash me!" In hindsight, they weren't really Bible-bashing me, that's just how I perceived it at the time. Meanwhile, outside of my home, I had several encounters with people, strangers, who would approach me and tell me about Jesus. I always had a confident response – "I am a Hindu." I wasn't interested in changing or believing something else. But if I was really honest with myself, I was seeking for truth, whilst feeling a little lost. I was asking questions, and I wasn't getting the answers that I desired. But that was my battle and I didn't want anyone interfering with that.

At the time I worked in Bond Street, London. One evening I took the Central line to Ealing Broadway as usual, and upon exiting the station I was approached by a couple of young Christians. We had a brief conversation and I gave my usual response; they didn't seem phased by my abruptness and rather hollow responses. They asked me about the gods I believed in and asked about my salvation. I had no answer. I did say before I walked away that "I am happy, and Jesus is a "white-man-God." When I look back, I wonder at my typical teenage ignorance and sense of rebelliousness.

During this time I got to a point where I had no belief in any kind of meaningful path or religion. But I knew there was a God. I had spiritual questions that no one could answer. I continued my search for God and the deeper things of life in various beliefs: through my faith, by seeing a psychic, exploring astrology and transcendental meditation. I even had some surreal encounters such as out-of-body experiences, and I searched into colour therapy, auras and other new age ideas. But somehow, my soul and spirit was not satisfied. there was always a void. Yet I could see the faith rising in my parents, the change in them was still evident.

It was around 1994 and Shaneen invited me to come along to one of their Friday night youth groups. By this time my heart had softened and so I went. I didn't know what was going to happen – but something did. While I was there I couldn't help noticing the joy, the passion, and the laughter. Nobody had coerced these young people into coming along – they wanted to be there!

Shaneen gathered everyone into a circle to pray and I just allowed myself to be immersed into that atmosphere. Shaneen then prayed for me, and I felt God touch me. I felt His presence in such a tangible way that I knew in that moment that whatever I had been looking for all my life, I had just found it.

When she finished praying I went and sat down and felt God put His arms around me. Really, it was just like someone wrapping their arms around me, enveloping me. It was a tangible and heavy presence; imagine someone physical is standing next to or over you and you can feel their warmth, their body, their breath.

That's what I felt. God's presence around me that night was so real, and in an instant I received a supernatural revelation of Him and His love for me. I knew He was with me, and just sharing this now brings tears of joy and relief to me, even after all these years. I found God! I found God! The presence of God is what I had been seeking and craving so intensely and now I had found Him. The One who I had been longing for all my life. The questions didn't matter anymore; His presence gave me enough evidence to understand HE IS.

That night, I prayed and believed in my heart and became born again. As I am typing this I am touched by His love and mercy and tears are falling freely. I know now, how God had been knocking on the door of my heart all those years; and I realised that I had been asking, seeking and knocking earnestly too.

I was a God chaser. Now I had caught Him, I was not letting go.

CHAPTER TWO

The Sapphire and the Warrior Part One

> *Then Adonai Elohim said, "It is not good for the man to be alone. Let Me make a well-matched helper for him." Genesis 2:18 (TLV)*

I believe that there is someone God has chosen for you to share your life with. This is how I found the one God chose for me.

It was March 2000. I had come back to the UK after working in Manhattan, New York, and was looking for work. A banking software company based in Westminster offered me a job, quite different from my previous roles, but the opportunity arose and I took it.

It was my second day at work, and I saw a tall, tanned, good-looking guy walk onto the floor I worked on. He was about my age, with a long, confident stride, and I looked at him twice. He did a double take too and didn't hide it. I remember thinking, "He's fit," and later learned he thought the same about me. Well, he later admitted the actual words that went through his head were, "Who is that dark haired pretty thing?"

I moved offices shortly afterwards, so didn't expect to see him again. But then one day in July, this same young man walked in. We both looked at each other and I knew he was "checking me out" – and he knew I was doing the same. I found out his name was Gary.

I laugh when I think about it now, because I was not interested in getting into a relationship with anyone at that point. It was me and God and that was all I needed.

Nevertheless, Gary and I got on well enough to share a few lunches, and we remember talking about Genesis, Adam and Eve, and God. I cannot remember how this conversation happened, but I do remember thinking that he was definitely searching. This early attraction turned into a love-hate relationship as we got to know each other better. I found him arrogant and he found me challenging in the work place. And so, nothing happened until one December evening.

It was the office Christmas party, which started with a lunch at Planet Hollywood in Piccadilly Circus, followed by a West End matinee show, and then drinks at a bar for those who wanted to continue into the evening.

At the theatre our company had been allocated a block of seats, but within that block we could sit where we wanted. I ended up between Gary and another colleague, who by this time was in a drunken stupor and very quickly fell asleep – there's always one isn't there?

The person sitting in front of me blocked my view of the stage a little so I needed to look around them to see the action. I didn't fancy leaning into the snoozing colleague, so I asked Gary, "Can I lean over slightly?" Sounds cheesy I know, but I was being genuine – seriously!

Well, I don't know what happened, but there were sparks flying galore. I do believe that if I could have seen into the spiritual realm there would have been an array of fireworks going off – it must've been like bonfire night. It felt like something out of a romantic novel, I really could sense and feel this charge of electricity between us. My tummy began to have little flutters and I think there may have been an angelic host standing over us, because I had never felt this before, not this intense chemistry and attraction.

We were fully aware of each other's presence, and after a while Gary put his arm around me. Yes I know! Weird huh? Given the antagonism we'd been feeling towards each other! But for some reason it seemed the most natural thing to do. We continued enjoying the show, whilst wondering about this unexpected – but beautiful and strange – connection that was being made. I think even now, after many years, it was a phenomenon.

After the show, the majority of us went on to a bar. Gary decided he wanted to stay close to me and if I am honest I wanted to be close with him too. But I remembered my focus on God and, to Gary's disappointment, decided to go home.

The week that followed, we began to exchange more intimate small talk and share quiet moments at work. I remember feeling shy and excited, yet trying to be cool at the same time. Gary and I were flirting with each other and the attraction wasn't fading, so one Wednesday morning he came to my desk and suggested going on a date that evening. A group of our colleagues were going for drinks in Covent Garden, celebrating breaking up for the Christmas holidays, so we decided we would watch an early movie then join them.

Anyway, he walked away from my desk and I immediately began to have doubts. I kept thinking about how I could cancel on him. It was December – I remembered I had an appointment for a blood test with the nurse at my local GP at the same time Gary and I were due to meet in Leicester Square. I knew if I cancelled the appointment I would not have my tests done until the New Year, and I would rather have got it out of the way. Feeling good about letting him down with a genuine excuse I decided, "That's it, I am going to just meet him at Covent Garden with everyone else."

Later that morning I went to the ladies' toilets to pray – I had been fasting that morning for a cousin and I would usually spend time in prayer when I had a few moments.

I locked myself in, knowing there was no one else on this side of the building that was likely to interrupt me. I prayed silently, quietly interceding for my cousin and dwelling on other things on my heart.

As I finished and said, "Amen" I heard a voice, "Call your doctor."

I looked around the cubicle, I knew no one had come into the ladies.

The voice spoke again, "Call your doctor."

It was a small, quiet voice, but one that spoke assertively.

It dawned on me I had just heard the voice of God for the first time!

I came out of the cubicle, part of me still looking to see if anyone was there and lo, there wasn't. I went straight to my desk and called the surgery. I said, "This is Neelam Gill."

The receptionist said, "Ah, Miss Gill, we have been trying to call you. The nurse is off sick, we will have to rebook your blood test for the New Year."

I put the phone down, looked up to heaven and said, "God, why do you want to send me on a date with this man?" In my heart I was thinking, surely dates are not something that come from God. What did I know about how God arranges things? He truly works in mysterious ways and dating was clearly permitted.

So, I had no excuse to give to Gary, and we met to go to the cinema as agreed. We watched *Meet the Parents*, which now seems uncanny, but thoroughly enjoyed it. I hadn't told anyone from the office we were meeting beforehand, not even my friend Sam, who was surprised to see us walk into the bar together. She took me aside and said, "You look like you're in love, like you are meant to be together."

I was still trying to act cool about it, so responded with, "Nah, he's not my type, I am not really that interested." I had invited one of my close friends, Met, to meet us at the bar as she lived in Covent Garden. She said something similar: "Wow, he's really into you, you look like you have a connection."

"Oh, I don't know Met," I replied as we stood outside the bar having a girly chat about connections and guys. I was clearly showing signs of uncertainty about this budding relationship, but Met's response to this was a quiet, "We'll see."

The truth is, part of me was keen, but another part of me was not. In fact, there was someone else outside of work who had been showing interest – he was just a little more my type, or so I thought.

My relationship with God was so satisfying I did not feel insecure or needy in any way. Even though I had much to learn about spiritual things, I felt that God was quenching my hunger and thirst. But God had other plans!

CHAPTER THREE

The Sapphire and the Warrior Part Two

Adonai Elohim built the rib, which He had taken from the man, into a woman. Then He brought her to the man. Genesis 2:22 (TLV)

"So, what are you doing for the Christmas holidays?" I asked Gary, already thinking I was going to miss him.

"Driving down to Brighton after work and will be there till I go skiing with a few friends. What are you up to tonight?"

"It was my cousin's birthday a few days ago, so we have planned a girly night. My friend Met has got us on to the guest list for a few places so we'll be out in London having a fab night."

Later, I went to Gary's desk to say goodbye before I left to go home, noticing I was feeling a little empty and gutted. I had clearly begun to like him and to enjoy his company. If I'm honest, by this time I really fancied him.

When I reached home, I started planning the night: clothes, timing and phone calls. I rang my cousin to check details but there was no answer – she had gone AWOL, absent without leave. I called her friend and she had not been able to contact her either.

I called Met to discuss what to do and we decided we would wait to hear from her. Then I tried my cousin again – still no answer. It rapidly became obvious that something else had come up for her, so we called the evening off. We found out the next day that she had, indeed, been distracted and her mobile phone battery had died too. So, there I was, at a loose end. Funny that.

The house phone rang. I thought it might be my cousin at last, but no, it was Billy, a friend from church. "Nee, I have been trying to get hold of you, I have a word from God for you." I was curious of course, but still a little distracted by the unravelling of my evening plans. "I have been trying to email you, but it kept bouncing back. Is blah blah your email address?" Billy asked. I replied that he had it right and we both wondered why his messages hadn't come through.

Everything is about timing with God. I enquired inquisitively, "So what is this word?" He said to me, "What are you looking for? A gold ring, or a gold mine?"

I was stumped. "Uh? Not sure, I don't get what you are asking me, Billy." It felt like a test.

Billy explained, "God is saying you are looking for a gold ring, but He wants to give you a gold mine. The gold ring is shiny, sparkly and good to look at, and it is precious, but what God wants to give you is a gold mine. The gold mine does not appear to be much, but when you dig deep, you will get so much gold and so many precious stones, and it will just keep coming as you keep digging."

I asked Billy what this might be referring to. He replied without hesitation. "A husband."

I knew in my spirit this message was about Gary and my heart leapt. But how could I know this was about Gary? Somehow I just did.

I put the phone down, feeling special that God was speaking to me, and amazed at how He was now orchestrating things.

As I pondered this for a few moments I heard that same voice that I heard in the ladies cubicle at work:

"Call Gary."

This time I actually responded to the voice.

"I don't know his number and besides he is on his way to Brighton." I then thought, "Oh my gosh, I am questioning God! How did I do that?"

These were the days before most of us had mobile phones; Gary didn't have one, and I didn't know his home number.

I felt the prompt again. "Call Gary." But I didn't have his home number! Then I recalled that he had been working from home that Monday, and I'd needed to call him about something – I had dialled his number then.

I looked at the digits on the phone and tried to remember what I had dialled. The number came to me easily and at the first try. I think an angel must have stood beside me, directing my fingers to the correct buttons.

The phone rang. I felt so silly and stupid because: one – I did not know if this was the right number; two – Gary hadn't given me his number and wouldn't be expecting a call; three – Gary was likely not at home; four – even if he was, he may think it was presumptuous of me to call him; and to top it off, I had told him about our well-planned girly night for my cousin's birthday. Nevertheless I was going to be obedient to the voice.

The phone was ringing, and lo and behold, Gary answered. That deep, smooth voice said, "Hello." I instantly felt shy and didn't know what to say. I couldn't say, "God told me to phone you" – well not yet anyway! Gary had left the office late and decided to leave for Brighton in the morning. He asked about my night out and I explained how my cousin had gone AWOL so the rest of us had decided to postpone it. Unexpectedly, we were both free.

We agreed to meet in Ealing Broadway, which was about half way between our homes. My brother and his wife happened to be driving there for their Christmas night out, more synchronicity. So I arranged to meet Gary in one of the bars and hopped in the car with them.

What timing, eh? God makes things so easy and effortless.

After a quick drink in Ealing, Gary and I drove to Chiswick, where we sat in Café Rouge, talking and talking some more and drinking hot chocolate. It was amazing. I couldn't believe how much I really liked him. I could tell he felt the same. The love-hate part of our relationship was truly over.

Hours passed and we reluctantly returned to the car. We sat in it on Chiswick High Road and talked some more, because we didn't want the night to end. He had to keep the engine running for some time to keep us warm. We both agreed, "This feels so right, like we've known each other for years." It started to snow, fluffy white flakes falling from a clear, starry sky. I just have to say this was God's way of giving us an uber-romantic night, huddled together talking, and just being in Gary's metallic gold Rover 25. It was not an expensive restaurant or noisy bar, it was perfect.

Just thinking about it makes me feel loved in so many ways, and I feel a little emotional, in a good way, as I reminisce about that night. God is so romantic; He set the most idyllic scene for His chosen vessels.

It was this night that I knew we were meant to be together.

But I daren't say anything, certainly not yet anyway.

This is how our relationship began. A relationship hand-picked by God Himself, orchestrated by Him and to this day sealed by Him.

The words "Call your doctor" and "Call Gary" led me to my divine marital destiny.

I now know the time I spent at this company was a divine appointment. As well as meeting Gary, there were countless godly encounters, including a prophetic dream-like premonition which led my friend Sam to a special church event where she accepted Jesus into her life, becoming born again and experiencing spiritual joy and laughter. All I know is that God will lead you down paths and to places where you will be blessed, and also be a blessing.

Neelam means sapphire. Gary means warrior.

Gary and I were married 19th February 2006.

This is how I see it. When God brought Eve to Adam, He walked her down the aisle in Eden and presented her to Adam, like an earthly father walking his daughter down the aisle. The best gift Adam received was being built while he was sleeping!

CHAPTER FOUR

Love in the Storm

The one who does not love has not become acquainted with God [does not and never did know Him], for God is love. [He is the originator of love, and it is an enduring attribute of His nature.] 1 John 4:8 (AMP)

We have come to know [by personal observation and experience], and have believed [with deep, consistent faith] the love which God has for us. God is love, and the one who abides in love abides in God, and God abides continually in him. 1 John 4:16 (AMP)

It was a Saturday lunch time and I was about to drive back home from a client session, a trip of about fifteen minutes.

I got in my car and started my journey home, unaware of what was going to happen in just a few moments. All of a sudden I started to feel God's presence all around me in the car. The car was filled with a heavy, tangible His presence; it was filled with His love which surrounded me. All I could do was cry, I cried so much, but I wasn't sad, I was overwhelmed with this unconditional love that I could not fathom or understand. I was undone.

God began to remind me about how much He loved me with images and visions from when I was born to that day and beyond. I saw flashbacks of my life, moments where He was there and involved.

Typing this is bringing hot tears to my eyes, and as I am sitting in a bar in the Maldives I am trying to keep my focus so I do not get anyone's attention. God was telling me and showing me how much He loves me. I felt overcome and special, yet I know this is how much He loves each one of His creations and many will live and die not knowing.

He reminded me of many things, and brought to mind things I had forgotten or possibly hadn't recognised as His love for me.

I began to recollect my life from a baby to the present, things that happened along the way, some which may have seemed insignificant, but God was showing me how He had been present and loved me with an everlasting love that I truly couldn't contain, and it was bubbling up inside of me. I felt like I was going to explode. Maybe this is what "my cup running over" feels like? I saw my life in a different way to how I had perceived it before; I saw God's fingerprint and His divine orchestration.

When I reached home, I climbed out of my car, leaving it unlocked, and ran in the house. Gary was in the garden and when he realised I was home he came in to see me in floods of tears and, worried, asked, "What's wrong?"

When I didn't respond he put his arm around me, sat me down and then asked again, "What's wrong, has anything happened?"

I blurted out, "It's God! He just loves me so much!"

After calming down, I was able to explain what had just happened in the car. I later comprehended this very real, tangible experience in the car, it was a conversation where God was doing all the talking. It would become an anchor for me, a place I could go back to when I needed reminding of His love for me. This was my altar – it prepared me for what was coming next. God loves us with an everlasting love and His thoughts towards us are innumerable. His Word says in Psalm 139:

For you formed my inward parts;
you knitted me together in my mother's womb.
I praise you, for I am fearfully and wonderfully made.
Wonderful are your works; my soul knows it very well.
My frame was not hidden from you,
when I was being made in secret,
intricately woven in the depths of the earth.

Your eyes saw my unformed substance;
in your book were written, every one of them,
the days that were formed for me,
when as yet there was none of them.
How precious to me are your thoughts, O God!
How vast is the sum of them!
If I would count them, they are more than the sand.
I awake, and I am still with you.
Psalm 139:13–18 (ESV)

In the Bible, multiple scriptures speak of God's unfailing love for us, even when circumstances around us do not make sense. Here are just three of them:

> *The LORD your God is in your midst, a mighty one Who will save; He will rejoice over you with gladness; He will quiet you by His love; He will exult over you with loud singing. Zeph 3:17 (ESV)*

> *There is no fear in love, but perfect love casts out fear. For fear has to do with punishment, and whoever fears has not been perfected in love. 1 John 4:18 (ESV)*

> *But, in all these things we are more than conquerors through Him who loved us. For I have been persuaded that neither death nor life, nor angels nor rulers, nor present circumstances nor things coming, nor powers, nor height nor depth, nor any other creation, will be able to separate us from the love of God which is in Messiah, Yeshua our Lord. Romans 8:37–39 (ONM)*

Verses like these have given me a solid foundation to stand on during times of difficulty and uncertainty. These are not just letters and words—these are God-breathed words. If they can help me, they can help you. I did not know what was coming, but God had spoken. I was being perfected by His love for me. He was telling me in the most profound encounter how much He loves me.

CHAPTER FIVE

Ectopic Episode

Even if He slays me, I will wait for Him; I will surely defend my ways before Him." "Yet I know that my Redeemer lives, and in the end, He will stand on earth. Job 13:15; 19:25 (TLV)

Monday morning, about a week after my Saturday encounter with God in the car, I said to Gary, "I think I am pregnant." We did a pregnancy test and it came up positive. We were so excited and happy. I said to Gary, "I have had some pain on the right side, I thought they were my monthly cycle pains, but if I'm pregnant, they can't be – perhaps we should see the doctor?"

We booked an emergency appointment that day. The GP said he thought I might have an ectopic pregnancy – I had never heard of this term before, I didn't worry and just went with the flow. He said to go straight to the hospital, which we did. Everything was like a whirlwind.

This wasn't our first visit to the hospital that week. A few days before we had had a terrible night; my father had been rushed to the Accident and Emergency department and had almost died. The doctors resuscitated him and bought him back to life, but he was very poorly so they transferred him to the Intensive Care Unit. We could not see him until the following day. When I did visit, he spoke to me of things I do not wish to share publicly, but I knew my dad had a very real spiritual experience. He said he saw the doctors and nurses trying to resuscitate him and he heard himself praying. We both knew that God was keeping a promise to him. I will never forget what my dad and I understood that day; all we concluded was that God and heaven are real, and salvation was promised to our household.

So as we arrived at the hospital with our own problems, I was still worried about my dad. I knew he was upstairs in ICU and there I was, being admitted downstairs. After being examined by a doctor, I learned that "ectopic" meant that the embryo had got stuck in my fallopian tube, and although they could see it was "healthy" they would have to remove it to prevent another ectopic pregnancy occurring in that tube. Even if one fallopian tube was damaged, I could still fall pregnant naturally as the second tube looked healthy. My mind was on my dad, and so I didn't really get a chance to comprehend what had happened, and being positive and a woman of faith I did not let it consume me.

After six weeks of praying for my dad to be well and for a miracle to take place, he passed away from this life to be with His Lord. God spoke to me in the corridor of the hospital the day the doctors said they could do nothing more. He said, "Either way, you win" and in a moment I fully understood – whether my dad pulled through or passed away, we won! In God we never lose! What revelation and love God promises.

Shortly after, we travelled to Cyprus. My sister was getting married out there and my father had clearly instructed us to continue with plans for the wedding. This was a great time of healing, we laughed and cried and created many memories together. It was truly a holiday my dad would have loved. I returned from Cyprus pregnant, but didn't actually realise until a few weeks later. I could sense I was having a baby – I now understand this sixth sense that women have. I took the pregnancy test and it came up positive. I was so happy, scared and excited at the same time. I told Gary and we shared the news a couple of days later with my family. This was like a breath of fresh air since we were still grieving our father passing away – a new life. I had no pain! Not like before.

But late one night, I came home and felt surges of pain run through my side. The pain felt like contractions, but I wasn't sure. I went to the bathroom thinking maybe I needed to relieve myself.

The pain came again and I screamed really loudly. Next thing, I was running through fields, the sky was blue and I could hear myself running and laughing so much, almost like a little girl. I had not a care in the world, no fear or pain. The field was tall grass or wheat, I can't quite place what it was, but it was like heaven.

When I opened my eyes I saw Gary's face close to mine, with wide worried eyes. He had caught me before I fell and carried me to the bed. I was lying there, in so much pain and it felt like life was slipping away from me. I called out to God, "Is this it? Have I done enough for Gary, for my family, for clients, for the world?" I set myself right with God as I felt life draining from me. Suddenly I heard a loud clear voice saying, "No."

While this was happening, Gary was on the phone to the emergency services, asking for an ambulance. A short while later it arrived and we were taken to the hospital. I had another ectopic pregnancy. This time it had ruptured and I had begun to haemorrhage internally. I recall the doctor explaining their priority was to save my life, and therefore they would need to remove the other fallopian tube. A third death. Another baby. I could not believe it.

On the third day I got up, walked to the window of the hospital room and said, "I am alive and as Jesus rose on the third day to a new resurrected life, I too am rising from this." I felt determined to not let this overtake my life.

During the weeks that followed, as I was convalescing, I went back to my altar, where God displayed His unconditional deep love for me in the car, and I knew in my spirit I was going to be OK. We were going to be OK.

My God is faithful; even if I don't always understand things, I know He loves me and Gary, and He has a good plan for us. I know one day we will be united with our children.

I am alive and I have my health. The legacy and memory of my father lives on. All is well.

> *Naked came I out of my mother's womb, and naked will I return there: the LORD gave, and the LORD has taken away; blessed be the name of the LORD. Job 1:21 (ONM)*

CHAPTER SIX

Moving My Mountain

Truly I say to you that whoever would say to this mountain, "You must immediately be removed and you must immediately be cast into the sea," and would not doubt in his heart but would believe that what he is saying is happening, it shall be to him. Mark 11:23 (ONM)

I felt sick, like I was going to vomit violently. I felt defeated, scared and overwhelmed, and simply sick to the pit of my stomach at the numbers in front of me.

I was sitting at my desk, Gary opposite me looking overwhelmed; we had just calculated our total amount of debt. I am too embarrassed even to share in this book what the figure was, but let me tell it was more than forty thousand pounds.

The truth was staring us in the face and no matter how many excuses we came up with to justify this dreadful fact (oh and trust me, we had some really good excuses!) we knew that this was a burden we did not want to carry anymore. More importantly, our God said we are not be slaves or to be in debt, we are to be lenders and not borrowers. I concluded that if I earned one thousand pounds per month in addition to what I brought in normally, I could pay the debt off in a reasonable time. This was my thinking and logic, my earthly wisdom – but God had another plan.

He said, "My ways are higher than your ways." And thank God they are!

I began to take this burden to God, praying, "Increase my income so I can pay this debt. Forgive me!"

Shortly after this, in October 2011, I heard a recording of a sermon by a well-known preacher, titled "Speak to Your Mountain." The basis of the sermon was Jesus' comparison of a problem or difficulty with having a mountain in your life. It could be anything that stands in the way of you and your blessing or destiny with your Creator. His instruction is not to avoid, describe, or get around the mountain, but speak to it – to tell it to go, to get out – to "be lifted up and thrown into the sea" (Mark 11:23).

When I heard this sermon it was as though I absorbed it. I ingested the word like food! It nourished and fulfilled me. I listened to the recording repeatedly and changed the tone and content of my prayers. I followed the instruction given in the scripture. Jesus said, "Speak to your mountain." He also said, "I am the Bread of Life." God's Word was the solution that became my daily bread.

I started to "tell this mountain where to go" – it had no authority to be in our life. Each morning I would wake up and kick this mountain out of the door. I would literally kick my legs in the air, as if kicking this invisible but very real mountain. It sounds bizarre, but I know God works in mysterious ways! So actually this is quite normal.

Gary went off to work and I would start shouting at this "unseen" mountain.

If you had walked in to my home on those mornings you would have wondered, "Who is Neelam arguing with?" I did this almost every day, or as much as I could. I had so much passion to be debt free. I declared the promises of God and reminded the mountain of debt that it was an illegal alien; it had no right to be in our life. I was like the persistent widow, whom Jesus spoke of in a parable in the gospel of Luke chapter 18. This widow kept going to the judge, asking, seeking, knocking. I kept going to God, speaking His Word to the mountain I was faced with.

In February 2012 Gary and I became debt free and, to top that off, we flew off to Cuba for an amazing holiday! I did not have to work my fingers to the bone or take years to pay it off. My heavenly Father did it. All I needed to do was have faith the size of a mustard seed and stand with the authority that God had given me through Jesus and He delivered me and Gary from bondage like the Israelites were delivered from the house of bondage in Egypt.

Mediate, chew, digest, ponder, and above all, have faith. Faith the size of a mustard seed.

The mustard seed is one of the smallest seeds, yet scripture tells us that, if we have faith this size, we can move mountains. We can move obstacles from our life, whether a financial crisis, a legal entanglement, people making unprovoked trouble, or anything that keeps you from living the abundant God-centred life. I add a caveat to this though – remember that we often make our own beds, and so there are times when we must live with the consequences of our decisions and actions. In my case, I had to say sorry and make a commitment to be wise.

The Parable of the widow, read and consider how this speaks to you:

> *Then Yeshua told them a parable to show that they should always pray and not be discouraged, He said, "There was a judge in a certain city who neither feared God nor respected people. And there was a widow in that*

city who kept coming to him, saying, 'Give me justice against my opponent. "He was unwilling at the time. But afterward he said to himself, 'Although I don't fear God or respect people, yet because this widow keeps bothering me, I will give her justice so she won't wear me out by her incessant coming.'" Then the Lord said, "Hear what the unjust judge is saying. Won't God do justice for His chosen ones, who cry out to Him day and night? Will He be slow to help them? I tell you, He will quickly give them justice. But when the Son of Man comes, will He find faith on the earth?" Luke 18:1–8 (TLV)

Today we are still debt free and plan to always live as God wills, to be lenders, to be the head. I know whatever mountains are in your way, by faith and by declaring the living Word of God, the mountain(s) will have to go! The mountain will have to obey the Creator's words, not my words, but the scripture that I proclaimed. The Word is the truth and the truth sets you free. Speak to your mountain today!

The Lord will open to you His good treasure, the heavens, to give the rain to your land in its season, and to bless all the work of your hand. You shall lend to many nations, but you shall not borrow. And the Lord will make you the head and not the tail; you shall be above only, and not be beneath, if you heed the commandments of the Lord your God, which I command you today, and are careful to observe them. Deuteronomy 28:12–13 (NKJV)

CHAPTER SEVEN

My Promised Land

But you have come to Mount Zion—to the city of the living God, the heavenly Jerusalem, and to myriads of angels, a joyous gathering. Hebrews 12:22 (TLV)

So then you are no longer strangers and foreigners, but you are fellow citizens with God's people and members of God's household. Ephesians 2:19 (TLV)

I have been procrastinating about writing the last few chapters of this book, but today I am being obedient and I'm going to finish it. It's funny, the very things that matter most or create impact are the ones that get put to the back of the list.

As I sit here in a café in Gerrard's Cross, reading through what I have written, tears roll down my face, my heart is pounding and the passion to share my story and conversations with God rise up. God willing, I will finish this.

It's not that I am superior or better than anyone. In God's eyes we are all His beloved and special. But I do know that we all have a story and deep experience of life, and we each have a unique way to share that with others.

I have had many conversations with God and have heard His voice clearly. As a believer this is not unusual, this should be our normal experience, but I know God does not only speak to believers, He speaks to everyone, we are just too distracted to hear Him. I am certain God has spoken to me many more times than I have acknowledged or realised.

From my experience to date, I hear from God in the following ways:

• His audible voice.

• His Word.

• A visible sign, which is either a confirmation or follows with confirmation.

• A vision – a clear open vision, like a movie, and prophetic words from His people and others.

• A divine revelation to my spirit of knowledge and understanding.

If God can use a donkey to speak (read about this in the book of Numbers 22:28–30) then He will use all His creation to speak, including nature around us (there are many scriptures speaking of this, such as Psalms 95 and 96). He will also give us a very strong discernment, which is like intuition or inner knowledge. There are many times my Father has communicated to me, and I feel honoured to have that relationship with Elohim, the Creator. This is something we all can have – including you.

So to my next encounter.

Gary and I were preparing our home for sale and we had a real sense that where He was going to take us now was going to unleash the next level of our life and divine assignment.

It was March 2013, the house went up for sale, and within 24 hours we had a viewing. The agent called to book the viewing in, and he explained a little more about this potential buyer.

On the day of the viewing, Gary and I were in the study. The agent bought her to meet us as she had a couple of questions.

As she was standing there I could see her living in the house. I heard the voice of God saying, "She is going to buy this home." Before the close of business that day, she put an offer in with the agent, and he said to her, "Why don't you sleep on it?" The next morning she increased the offer and the agent presented it to us. We were told she was a cash buyer, chain free!

We moved to our current home in June 2013. One day, within a short time of being here, and while I was tidying up, the Lord spoke to me. I wasn't in prayer or anything, He just spoke, "Wherever you go, I will be there," which caused me to stop in my tracks. Typing this brings tears to my eyes, the thought that the God of all creation loves us enough to speak so clearly and give us a promise. Instantly I received understanding. He was telling me that wherever Gary and I go, any home, any place, He will be there with us. What immense assurance and security is that? I felt totally loved and humbled.

It was actually two years later that I read Joshua chapter one, and when I did, I cried so much. For I knew that I wasn't making things up in my own mind, this is exactly what the Lord was telling me that day.

> *"Be strong! Do not be terrified or dismayed, for ADONAI your God is with you wherever you go." Joshua 1:9 (TLV)*

In fact, as I am reading the chapter yet again and typing this, I am realising that I wasn't hearing fully – the instruction and promise of Joshua chapter 1 was the message the Lord was giving that day for us. I am even more humbled.

You see, God often speaks in the same language of Scripture, His Word – His Living Word! I have never forgotten His direct and personal word to me – to us – that wherever we go, He will be there. I know in my spirit that He was saying that His presence will be in my home, wherever we call home. His presence was in the home we sold, and is in the home we are in now.

I don't believe in coincidences. I call them "Godincidences." I don't believe in luck or karma. I know that I don't need to earn my way to heaven or into a relationship with God, I just have to believe and take that position as a daughter of the King. Where we are now is where I have experienced much of God's presence and glory – His divine presence dwelling with us – and I do believe in the not-too-distant future another home will be provided, my promised land.

In June 2015 again, whilst I was pottering in the guest bedroom, I heard the voice of God: "Come to Israel for Yom Kippur." I thought, "Wow Lord, you want us to come to Israel. Again!" I was quite excited – we had been there two years before. I love Israel, my heart is there. I checked myself, was it my voice? Yet I knew it wasn't. Well, I can confirm it wasn't as I knew I wouldn't have used the words "Yom Kippur."

I told Gary and spoke with our pastors, telling them that I had heard from the Lord. I began to look into the costs, but then "parked" it. I knew deep down I was seeking a confirmation, as the Bible also talks about a second witness or confirmation of things. In August a woman of God visited our home. She was a prophetess, someone who can speak of future events and offer words of knowledge. We had never met and she didn't know us, but she began to prophesy over Gary and me. She said, "The Lord has called you to Israel, you must go, it's a divine appointment." I had my second confirmation and we began preparation for the trip.

Sharing the details of the trip is perhaps destined for another book! But I will say it was truly a divine appointment and God showed up and really spoke to us. I want to encourage you, if you have not heard from God, call out to Him and ask Him to make Himself known, ask Him to speak. I know God is faithful – He will speak and He will show and direct you.

If you have been a believer and haven't heard, all I can say is think of a radio – in order to listen to your favourite station you need to get the right frequency and tune in, which also means tuning everything else out. If you are in between frequencies or stations sometimes it comes through fuzzily, with interference, and you can sometimes hear a little of two different stations.

Distractions, noise, busyness; these can be major obstacles, but once you are tuned in, even when you are tidying up, you can hear from Him!

When we left for Israel during September 2015, as I sat on the plane, I anticipated an encounter and confirmation of things. I expected a heavenly revelation and my God did not fail. He moved, showed and spoke. I knew if we are invited to His table it would be a feast!

> *That's plain enough, isn't it? You're no longer wandering exiles. This kingdom of faith is now your home country. You're no longer strangers or outsiders. You belong here, with as much right to the name Christian as anyone. God is building a home. He's using us all—irrespective of how we got here—in what he is building. He used the apostles and prophets for the foundation.*

Now he's using you, fitting you in brick by brick, stone by stone, with Christ Jesus as the cornerstone that holds all the parts together. We see it taking shape day after day—a holy temple built by God, all of us built into it, a temple in which God is quite at home. Ephesians 2:19-22 (MSG)

CHAPTER EIGHT

My Mirror

The Bible, the whole Bible, the Old Testament and New Testament, is the Word of God and He speaks to us through His Word, confirming and affirming things, revealing truth, wisdom and mysteries. The Word is a living Word. No matter when you read it, it is alive, and it is breathing.

A person in the year 1019AD reading the Bible will experience its relevance and power just as someone reading it in the year 2019! They will experience its significance and meaning to their life and situation at that time. God's Word is timeless and never goes out of fashion; it is the ultimate guidebook for life. I often refer to it as the "Manufacturer's Manual," others describe it as "Basic Instructions Before Leaving Earth."

The Bible tells us that God watches over His Word, to ensure it is performed. I guess even though there are many translations, I find comfort in knowing that God is watching over His Word and has provided me with exactly what I need, when I need it. As one who seeks Him, I know any further understanding I need will be provided and revealed at the appointed time.

There are many layers to the Word of God; some people have described it like an onion. I like to think that when the student is ready, the teacher appears to teach the next level. The Word of God is filled with love, wisdom, hope, prophecies (I call this God's intel), battles, life lessons, miracles, business intelligence, tests, as well as mysteries.

What I understand now is that our Father never holds back from revealing His Word and will. To get the best understanding when reading the Word:

• Read it in context and allow scripture to interpret scripture.

• Invite the Holy Spirit to guide, ask for understanding.

• Have a Hebraic mind-set, for me this has made a significant difference. What I mean by this is study the meaning of words in the original language, Hebrew, and you will gain a richer, deeper and truer meaning of the Word of God. Looking at biblical idioms with a Hebrew lens provides a better context within the culture at the time so that we can interpret God's Word more accurately. Note; our Messiah is Jewish and most of the writers of the Bible were Hebrew.

• Mediate on it, ponder it, mull over it, chew it, read again and again.

I also realised along the way that I can't just believe everything I am told or taught, I must be mature to go away and seek and test everything. Check the Word, does the teaching line up with the Word?

Here are some scriptures that have articulated my heart so perfectly and/or spoken to me in times of need, or trouble, or even as part of my reverence for YHWH (God) and as an ongoing promise for this life and through eternity. My feelings and understanding are much deeper than I can explain in this chapter, but I will share just a little. I am sure they will bless you too as you read them.

> *Blessed is the man who does not walk in the counsel of the ungodly, or stand in the way of sinners, or sit in the seat of the scornful. But his delight is in the Torah*

> *(Teaching) of the Lord and he mediates on His Torah (Teaching) both day and night. And he will be like a tree planted by the rivers of water that brings forth its fruits in its season, its leaf also will not wither and everything he does will succeed. Psalm 1:1-3 (ONM)*

One of my favourite psalms, which teaches me how not to behave, to meditate on His Word and as a result I shall be like a tree and that I will prosper in all that I do in ministry, in work, in life and in business. This has spoken to me on many occasions and has given me hope and faith when I needed it.

> *One thing that I have asked of the Lord, that I desire, that I would dwell in the House of the Lord all the days of my life, to behold the beauty of the Lord and to inquire in His temple. Psalm 27:4 (ONM)*

This psalm speaks so perfectly of my heart. When I first read it, I simply knew this was my heartbeat, my breath, and I began to understand my heart's hunger in a different way.

> *The Lord is my Shepherd, I shall lack nothing. He will cause me to lie down in green pastures. He will lead me beside the still waters. He will restore my soul; He will guide me in the paths of righteousness for His names sake. Yea, though I am walking through the valley of the shadow of death, I will be awed by no evil, for You are with me. Your rod and Your staff, they will comfort me. You will prepare, set, a table before me in the presence of my enemies. You have anointed my head with oil. My cup is running over. Surely goodness and loving kindness will pursue me all the days of my life and I will dwell in the house of the Lord forever. Psalm 23 (ONM)*

This tells me I don't have to be desperate for anything. If I am unwell, this is when the Lord is making me rest or be still so that I can be restored and refreshed. God is saying His presence is with me, even in dark times and He is the One that will bless me publicly. I don't need to chase anything but Him, but goodness and His love will chase me instead. When I feel I don't have enough, this reminds me that my cup actually runs over and I am able to be a blessing to others.

> *O God you are my God, early will I seek You. My soul thirsts for you, my flesh longs for You in a dry and thirsty land where there is no water to see Your power and glory, so I have seen You in the sanctuary. Because your loving kindness is better than life, my lips will praise You! Thus will I bless you while I live? I shall lift up my hands in Your name. My inner being will be satisfied as with marrow and fatness; and my mouth will praise You with Joyful lips when I remember You upon my bed and mediate on You in the night watches. Because you have been my Help, therefore I shall rejoice in the shadow of Your wings. My inner being follows hard after You. Your right hand upholds me.... But the king will rejoice in God. Everyone who swears by Him will glory, but the mouth of those who speak lies will be stopped. Psalm 63:1-9 (ONM)*

This psalm describes me at the deepest level and has often spoken to me in multiple situations. This is my psalm. This is my mirror.

> *For He is our peace, the One Who made both things into one and Who has loosed the dividing wall of the fence, cause of the enmity to His flesh, by His nullifying the tradition of the commandments by decrees, so that he*

> *could create the two, Jewish and non-Jewish into One New Man establishing peace so he could reconcile both in one body to God through the cross as God killed their enmity by means of Him, Y-shua. Ephesians 2:14-16 (ONM)*

This tells me that the glorious church or ecclesia is where both Jew and Gentile are reconciled and worshipping together. The dividing wall has come down through Jesus by what He did on the cross. It also tells me that in His congregation there is no rich or poor, free or slave, Jew or Gentile, no black or white, but we are all one in Messiah. He broke the bounds of man-made rules, traditions and decrees which have caused enmity over the years.

> *In the beginning God created the heavens and the earth. Genesis 1:1 (ONM)*

This has spoken to me many times. Just the power of "In the beginning God," sends shivers down my spine. I have discovered layers and layers from just the book of Genesis. No one can take my belief of creation away from me. My spirit and soul are completely in sync with this and I cannot explain how, but it is. I guess it's simply a divine connection and alignment.

This tells me how big my God is, and I truly cannot fathom Him. It skyrockets my reverence for Him. He truly knows me. He truly is.

> *And the Sprit and the bride are saying "You must come" and the one who hears must now say "You must come" and the one who thirsts must come faithfully, the one who wants must now take the water of life as a free gift. Revelation 22:17 (ONM)*

There is so much to understand and seek in this book, yet I hold on to the promise that Yeshua is returning quickly and my responsibility is to be a prepared bride, one that is watching out for His return one that has her garments ready. I look out for Him daily. Jesus our Messiah is coming again soon. He came the first time as a Lamb, to be the sacrifice for the whole world, but is coming again as the Lion of the tribe of Judah. "Come," I say ,"Come."

The Word is powerful; it is God's covenant-promise to us. It is like water to those who are thirsty, it is light to those who are struggling in darkness, it is the most delicious of delicacies that bring comfort to the soul, it is more valuable than precious stones, it is bread for nourishment, it is a weapon in times of trouble, it is a tool to solve problems and it is ointment that brings healing. It is Life.

CHAPTER NINE

My Prayer

Death and life are in the control of the tongue. Proverbs 18:21 (TLV)

I would like to share my heart's desire and prayer for you, my family, the nations of this world and for myself. In the beginning, when God created the heavens and the earth, it was with His words. He spoke the galaxy, planets, stars, into existence, and He said, "Let Us make man in Our image," and so, the earth and the universe as we know it was created. So as we are made in His image, likeness and carry His DNA, we also can create our tomorrow by speaking over it. This is a glimpse into my prayers – words that speak life.

For You

I pray you will find hope that there is a God and He truly is a God who hears and speaks. I pray you will have a personal encounter with your Creator, that you will hear Him when you call out to Him. I declare that you will know God intimately and you will come to know your identity in Him and have a supernatural revelation of His mysteries and revelation of the spiritual world and His will for you. May you know the difference between His voice and the voice of someone who may come disguised as an angel of light. May you be whole and fulfilled and understand that this life, as amazing and precious as it is, there is more beyond the grave. This life is a vapour and what lies ahead is eternal, may eternity be in your heart.

May you have the urge to seek the truth for yourself, for Scripture says, "Seek and you shall find, ask and it shall be given, knock and the door shall be answered" (Matthew 7:7). I declare you will receive the gift of salvation and know that what God has planned for you is something you will not even be able to comprehend. May you know His everlasting love for you and whatever you go through in this life, you will call upon your heavenly Father, and He will incline His ear to you and answer you. May you have many conversations with God and share them with others.

For This Nation

I pray this nation will stand united in love and truth, and will allow God to rule and reign and salvation will be our inheritance. I pray this nation will be a blessing to other nations and that the people will prosper in this land, that the homeless will find a home, the blind will see, the broken will be comforted, the lost will be found, the poor will rejoice, the rich will find salvation. I declare that people of all tongues and tribes will come together as one. I pray that even if there are differences that we will see the bigger spiritual and eternal picture and understand the blessing in what may look like a bad move because we believe in God and that He alone is sovereign.

I declare that Yeshua-Jesus, the Lion of Judah, will arise and roar and be a voice that brings people to pray together. I pray we will be a righteous nation that declares the works of the Lord and we will be a nation that stands with countries who are suffering at the hands of evil, we will be a light to many and will be strategic in taking this nation from glory to glory.

I pray we will be a nation that stands on its biblical foundation and will rise up to be an apostolic forerunner that is set apart but impacts the rest of the world for good. I pray we will be a nation that will stand with Israel and not divide Jerusalem the city of God, the special place where God chose to put His name. May we be a people who will not be deceived but keep watch of the signs.

For The World

For God so loved the world, that He gave His begotten Son, that whoever believes in Him, shall not perish but have everlasting life. John 3:16

May the God of heaven and earth come and rule in each person's heart and in their homes, bringing light and hope to every community. I pray for the peace of Jerusalem, the salvation of all Israel, one day they will say, "Blessed is He who comes in the name of the Lord!" May His will be done, His Kingdom come on earth as it is in heaven.

For My Family

I pray that every one of my family members will know their Creator and receive salvation. I pray each person will find peace that passes all understanding and be whole and be a mighty army for God, walking in His ways. I pray their life and soul shall prosper and they will be a light and blessing to many who their paths cross.

May we be a shining example to others, may love, truth and oneness in the Father be our foundation and way of life. May we enter into the rest and have no pressure to conform to the pattern of this world, but be the beautiful bold people we were born to be.

For Myself

I declare that I will do His will and be the salt and light in this world, and I will carry out each assignment fully by the leading of the Holy Spirit. I will walk in love, humility and boldness. I will stand like a tree planted by the rivers of water, and I will bear fruit in my season, my leaf shall not wither, and whatever I do shall prosper. I will not forsake my heritage as a daughter of the King and that I am blessed because of the covenant God made with Abraham. I will be a spotless bride and I shall dwell in the house of the Lord forever.

> *I will rejoice greatly in ADONAI. My soul will be joyful in my God. For He has clothed me with garments of salvation, He has wrapped me in a robe of righteousness—like a bridegroom wearing a priestly turban, like a bride adorning herself with her jewels. For as the earth brings forth its sprouts, and as a garden causes things sown to spring up, so ADONAI Elohim will cause justice and praise to spring up before all the nations. Isaiah 60:10-11(TLV)*

CHAPTER TEN

A Royal Invitation

Then you will call upon me and come and pray to me, and I will hear you. Jeremiah 29:12 (ESV)

Did you know that God is calling people every day to Himself? His invitation may not come on an embossed thick card in a gold envelope with a royal seal, through the letterbox; it may come in the most unusual, simple, uncommon, gentle, unassuming way. Just like the first coming of Jesus. He was the King of the universe but came as the passover lamb to be sacrificed for the world. Unpretentious, modest, unassuming and humble, but with a compelling purpose.

Your call could come as a voice, a dream, a feeling, a recurring wave of emotion, signs, strangers speaking, a quickening of the spirit, an awakening, a question, a thought, through Bible-believing loved ones, through creation or simply the silent void in your heart.

No matter how the invitation comes, I believe it will be like a love letter. A letter that is gently drawing and pulling you towards Himself—composed in the exact language and manner that captures your heart, mind and soul. After all, He knows you better than you know yourself.

Here is an example of how this letter might read:

Dear cherished one, you are called out of the world and into relationship with Me. You are called by Me for My purpose, which is a noble, honourable, and satisfying plan. Rejoice that you are called, as this call is irreversible and eternal. You have answered with joy at being chosen. You have dropped everything to answer My call and you have gladly turned from the world to Me. Therefore, when you call I will answer. I will be right there day and night, when you speak. When you call to Me, I will show you great and mighty things, which you could not imagine.

My call to come and follow Me is truly a love song sung to My Beloved. It is the rejoicing of My heart when the answer is, "yes." My proposal to my loved ones is continually going out. Let all who hear it say "yes" and come and follow Me.

God's call is like a marriage proposal. It is the highest calling any human could have. I said "yes" and He said "yes." Yeshua declared His love for me and gave me a covenant, a contract —the Ten Commandments, His Word and left me with a gift —the Holy Spirit—until He returns.

So why a "Royal" invitation? Because scripture reveals God's numerous names, revealing His Kingship and sovereignty— that He sits on a throne in Heaven. Yeshua is known as the King of kings, who will one day return to rule and reign. As sons and daughters of God the Father through the seed of Abraham we are in the royal bloodline. I encourage you to look into scripture for more on your identity as God sees it.

> *But you are a chosen people, a royal priesthood, a holy nation, a people for God's own possession, so that you may proclaim the praises of the One who called you out of darkness into His marvellous light. 1 Peter 2:9 (TLV)*

So how does one enter the kingdom of heaven? How is salvation obtained? Why Yeshua (Jesus), and who is He? What is this life walking with God? The following four scriptures answer these questions. However, for more in-depth understanding, read the Bible, the Word of God.

It speaks of salvation, the kingdom of heaven, God, Jesus, spiritual things and so much more. This is your Royal Invitation to seek and find. To enter into a new life, a royal line.

God Became Flesh

In the beginning was the Word; and the Word was with God, and the Word was God. He was with God in the beginning. All things came through Him, and there was not one thing that came into being without His participation. What had come in Him was life, and the life was the light of Mankind; and the Light shines in the darkness, nevertheless the darkness has not appropriated it. And the Word became flesh and lived among us, and we saw His glory, glory in the same manner as the only child of the Father, full of grace and truth. John 1:1–5,14 (ONM)

John the Baptist Testifies: The Lamb of God Revealed

The next day John saw Jesus coming toward him and said, "Look, the Lamb of God, who takes away the sin of the world! This is the One I meant when I said, 'A Man who comes after me has surpassed me because He was before me.' I myself did not know Him, but the reason I came baptizing with water was that He might be revealed to Israel." Then John gave this testimony: "I saw the Spirit come down from heaven as a dove and remain on Him. And I myself did not know Him, but the one who sent me to baptise with water told me, 'The Man on whom you see the Spirit come down and remain is the One who will baptize with the Holy Spirit.'" John 1:29-33 (ONM)

How to Enter the Kingdom of Heaven

Now there was a certain man among the Pharisees named Nicodemus, a ruler (a leader, an authority) among the Jews, who came to Jesus at night and said to Him, "Rabbi, we know and are certain that You have come from God [as] a Teacher; for no one can do these signs (these wonderworks, these miracles—and produce the proof) that You do unless God is with him." Jesus answered him, "I assure you, most solemnly I tell you, that unless a person is born again (anew, from above), he cannot ever see (know, be acquainted with, and experience) the kingdom of God." Nicodemus said to Him, "How can a man be born when he is old? Can he enter his mother's womb again and be born?" Jesus answered, "I assure you, most solemnly I tell you, unless a man is born of water and [even] the Spirit, he cannot [ever] enter the kingdom of God. What is born of [from] the flesh is flesh [of the physical is physical]; and what is born of the Spirit is spirit. Marvel not [do not be surprised, astonished] at My telling you. You must all be born anew (from above). The wind blows (breathes) where it wills; and though you hear its sound, yet you neither know where it comes from nor where it is going. So it is with everyone who is born of the Spirit." John 3:1-8 (AMPC)

Peter said to them, "You must immediately repent and each of you must immediately be immersed (baptised) in the name of Yeshua Messiah for forgiveness of your sins and you will take the gift of the Holy Spirit. For the promise is for you and for your children and for all those in far away places, whomever the Lord our God will call to himself" Acts 2:38-39 (ONM)

You can change your own destiny now, by accepting the invitation and truly believing and truly repenting, speaking and praying for salvation.

To be born again, first believe in the gospel - the good news that God sent His only Son, Yeshua the Messiah to save the world. He shed His blood to wash away all our sin, pain, curses and debts. He was the sacrificed Lamb of God, He paid the price for us all and through His atonement we can now be reconciled back to God our Creator.

> *for everyone who will call on the name of the Lord will be saved. Romans 10:13 (ONM)*

Here are four simple steps to help you follow Jesus:

1. Repent.

2. Believe.

3. Be baptised (in water and Spirit).

4. Live the born-again nature, walking as a disciple/follower.

Why not pray? I recommend you speak your heart, but here is an example:

Dear Heavenly Father, the Creator of the universe, today I believe You are real, you are a God that hears and speaks. Thank you for sending Your only begotten Son, Yeshua-Jesus Christ, to die for my sins on the cross and then rise to life again on the third day.

I invite You into my life, heart and soul to take full control. Forgive me for all my sins and wrongdoings, even things I may not have realised. I am truly sorry and ask You today to forgive me and wipe my slate clean. (You can also say "sorry" for specific things if you prefer – humility and surrendering all is vital.) *As I do this, I receive the free gift of salvation that I didn't have to earn, but by faith alone. Today, lead me by your Holy Spirit, show me how to now be baptised (fully immersed) without delay, and to follow you all the days of my life that my name will be written in the Book of Life.*

Thank You that all of my sin, shame, sickness and debt have been wiped away and You will remember them no more! Help me to live a righteous life by Your measure and not by the standard of this world. Help me to walk in Your truth all the days of my life and to hear from You and not by any other means that will cause me to stumble.

I ask this all in Yeshua-Jesus' name, Amen.

Date_____ (you can write the date here).

❖

Next Step

Begin speaking with Yeshua-Jesus daily. It is through an intimate relationship with Yeshua that you can come to God the Father, for they are One. Read His Word, the Holy Bible. Make a time to spend alone with Him daily, and develop intimacy as a newlywed husband and wife do. During this time, listen and meditate on a portion from His Word. Often we end up speaking so much we forget to breath, be still and listen also.

Find a local Bible-believing born-again Christian/Messianic congregation. You will need to be baptised (full immersion) and discipled (taught the Word of God from the Bible), and follow in the ways of Jesus Christ for He is our role model, the example. This beautiful and amazing event marks the beginning of a prophetic destiny for you, the angels in heaven are rejoicing now. God will be speaking with you in many ways, so keep your spiritual eyes and ears open.

You can ask the Holy Spirit to guide you to the right place and He will!

I have learned that this partnership, this relationship, is the single most fulfilling thing in the whole world – the whole universe; I wouldn't trade it for anything else. This walk is not easy, but through the storm you will have peace.

Through the difficulties He is with you. He will give you the desires of your heart according to His perfect will. I realise the desires of my heart must be aligned with His will so ask, and keep faith, the answer may not come as you expect. Stay steadfast (committed or unwavering) till the end, for your relationship with Yeshua-Jesus, is your exceedingly great reward!

EPILOGUE

I knew it was early, it was dawn, the sun had not come up yet. I was still half-asleep, but something was stirring within. I willed myself to go back to sleep, so I shut my eyes in an attempt to fall back into a blissful sleep. I then heard a gentle voice "come, walk with Me in the cool of the day."

I knew it was God. I felt so honoured and privileged, but I was so tired.

So I shut my eyes and told myself I will get up in a few minutes.

The voice came again.

"Come, and walk with Me in the cool of the day."

I knew this was not just any wake up call. This was an appointment. I knew somehow that God had something to say to me, and I was not going to miss this for anything.

I got up, went downstairs put on a big jumper and stuck on my wellies and walked into my garden.

To be continued

www.godandl.co.uk

www.ingramcontent.com/pod-product-compliance
Lightning Source LLC
LaVergne TN
LVHW021717080426
835510LV00010B/1006